The words of the wise and their dark sayings

(Book of Proverbs)

The proverb cannot be bettered

(Irish Proverb)

When a fool is told a proverb,
its meaning has to be explained

(Ashanti Proverb)

PROVERBS
&
SAYINGS
of
IRELAND

EDITED BY SEÁN GAFFNEY
& SEAMUS CASHMAN

WOLFHOUND PRESS

1995 anniversary edition, reprinted 1997
First published 1974 (hardcover). Paperback editions: 1976, 1978, 1979, 1982, 1985, 1986, 1990, 1992

Wolfhound Press
68 Mountjoy Square
Dublin 1

British Library Cataloguing in Publication Data

ISBN 0-86327-432-3

Cover design: Joe Gervin.
Cover illustration: 'Molly McCree' by Thomas Alfred Jones. Courtesy of the
National Gallery of Ireland.
Text illustrations: Robert Gibbings. Courtesy of the Artist's Estate, Laurence
Pollinger Ltd and Mercier Press.
Typesetting: Wolfhound Press.
Printed by the Guernsey Press Co Ltd, Guersney, Channel Isles.

CONTENTS

ACKNOWLEDGEMENTS

It is with particular pleasure that we welcome this 21st Anniversary Edition of *Proverbs & Sayings of Ireland*, and we are pleased to take this opportunity to thank the many thousands of readers who have purchased and, we trust, enjoyed this book down the years. We also acknowledge and thank Billy Merwick who provided the decorative illustrations (see example below) which enhanced all the previous editions of the book, and we congratulate him and wish every success for his exhibition of new paintings to be shown in Brussells also this year. The Robert Gibbings woodcuts chosen for this new edition wonderfully reflect the traditional and rural ethos of the proverbs themselves.

ACKNOWLEDGMENTS FROM THE FIRST EDITION

We acknowledge with gratitude the contributions and encouragement of many friends, in particular our parents, Ann and James Cashman, and Margaret Gaffney. A special word of thanks to Margaret Ryan, Deirdre Duffy, Monica Miller, Joy Adams, John Logue and Paul Walsh.

INTRODUCTION

The proverb cannot be bettered – Though the proverb is abandoned, it cannot be falsified – how true these are readers will best discover for themselves in the following collection of Irish proverbs, sayings and triads. The triad is perhaps the most fascinating type of saying and though little used today in the non-Irish speaking parts of the country, it is still to be heard in the Gaeltacht areas, in West Cork, Galway and the Aran Islands.

A glance through the index of key words reveals the range of the Irish proverb, its themes, and the imagery and symbols used. As might be expected, the reputed vulnerability of our race to religion and romanticism is well represented. But the story the proverb tells is not quite that of a priest-ridden peasantry content in their poverty. Rather it shows us to have – or at least to have had – a subtle, sly perhaps, but generally humorous self-confidence. 'The priest's pig' may get 'the most porridge'; but the proverb also advises us to be 'neither intimate nor distant with the clergy'! Nor are we shown to be wholly susceptible to romanticism: 'it's better to be lucky than to be an early riser' but 'there's no success without authority and laws'. The proverbs reveal a deep conviction in a relationship between the spiritual and the material that is both challenging and realistic.

Proverbs are, in a sense, a race's unconscious expression of its moral attitudes. Our proverbs seem frequently to take the form of a national confession of sins: the evils of drink, gambling, greed, vanity, improvidence abound. But the virtues are there: faith, gentleness, love of nature, tolerance, and a trust in a life after death that offers a constant check to the materialism already mentioned.

Irish proverbs are rich in nature symbolism and imagery: the wind, the sea, the mountains; plants, animals, birds and fishes. The kingfisher, mackerel, thistle, plover, the horse and the hare, even the common crow are all called upon to mirror our achievements, hopes and failings.

While the proverbs of a race are often readily identifiable as belonging to that race, the ideas expressed and the images used touch on matters more fundamental than a national identity. One can readily accept that Irish proverbs should have their exact counterparts among the proverbs of other Celtic races. There are numerous examples of similarities among the sayings of the Irish, Welsh and Scottish – A long illness doesn't lie (Irish); To be long sick and to die nevertheless (Welsh); Marriage at the dungheap and the Godparents far away (Irish); Marriage o'er the anvil, sponsorship o'er the sea (Scottish); A drink is shorter than a story (Irish and Manx); Bribery splits a stone (Scottish). Such typical proverbs as these listed here also have their counterparts in most European languages.

However, it is interesting to discover that our proverbs also have affinities with those of races as far distant as the West Indies and Africa. Among Jamaican people, who are of African descent, there is a saying: 'When you sleep wid darg, you ketch him flea'. Our equivalent is : 'He who lies with dog rises with fleas'. We speak of sending the goose on a message to the foxes' den; the Hausa of West Africa have: 'Even if the hyena's town is destroyed , one does not send a dog in to trade'.

Irish proverbs and sayings derive from two mainstreams: the gaelic tradition, in the Irish language, and the anglo-Irish tradition, in the English language. Both reflect the strong biblical influence found in the proverbs throughout 'western' countries. This collection includes some of the oldest seanfhocail (old sayings) recorded in Ireland as well as sayings of more recent origin. But it is by no means exhaustive. The exact origins of most of these sayings are unknown: perhaps a throw-away phrase; perhaps a line of a poem long forgotten – who knows? It is what survives that matters.

For readers interested in pursuing the Irish Proverb further, a brief word on some sources. Several substantial collections have been published (from which many in this collection have been taken, and which we gratefully acknowledge.) Most of these are unfortunately long out of print. The most recent, and certainly the finest is T. S. O'Maille, ed., *Sean-fhocala Chonnacht*, 2 vols. (Dublin, 1948-52). Others are: T.O'Donoghue, ed., *Sean-fhocail na Mumhain*, a Gaelic League publication, 1902; E. Ua Muirgheasa, ed., *Sean fhocla Uladh*, (1907) which contains English translations as does T.F. O'Rahilly, *A Miscellany of Irish Proverbs*, (Dublin 1922). Shorter collections will be found in J. O'Daly, *Irish Language Miscellany*, Burke, *Irish Grammar*; Hardiman, *Irish Minstrelsy*, 2 vols reissued by IUP in 1969; the *Gaelic Journal* and *The Ulster Journal of Archaeology*. P. W. Joyce , *English as we speak it in Ireland*, (Dublin 1910) is a useful and entertaining starting point though of limited use for proverbs. Two important sources still to be fully researched are the Douglas Hyde 'Diaries' in the National Library of Ireland, and the

9

manuscript collections of the Irish Folklore Department in UCD, in particular the 'Schools Mss.' for anglo-Irish proverbs. *Bealoideas* the journal of the Folklore Commission includes lists of proverbs in its various issues. Information on further sources will be found in bibliographies in the published works mentioned.

Most of the proverbs in this collection have been translated from the Irish language. English translations of proverbs in the Irish language are not always successful. We have endeavoured to remain as close to the original as possible. An illustration of the effects of translation, however, can be readily seen by comparing 'One beetle recognises another' with the original Irish proverb 'Aithníonn ciaróg ciaróg eile'. The impact of the expression depends greatly on the sound of the word ciaróg, and its repetition. The pattern cannot be reproduced satisfactorily in English; and the word 'beetle' is by comparison with the Irish word, weak and ineffectual.

We have classified each proverb by subject recognising that such classification is both limiting and subjective. For proverbs are by their very nature elusive and usually defy adequate classification under any one heading. However as the index contains the key-words of each proverb, our arrangement should cause the reader little difficulty.

Classifications

The proverbs are listed in this book alphabetically under the following headings. The Index of Key Words at the end of the book will guide the reader to specific proverbs.

Ability	Conversation	Fair-haired
Advice	Courtship	Fame
Affectation	Criticism	Familiarity
Age	Cunning	Fate
Anger	Curses	Fear
Appearance	Cynicism	Fighting
Art	Danger	Flattery
As....as...	Death	Flimsiness
Beauty	Debt	Food
Betrayer	Deception	Fool
Bitterness	Delusion	Foolishness
Blessings	Desire	Forgiveness
Boastings	Despair	Fortune
Borrowing	Devil	Frail
Bravery	Discipline	Freedom
Bribery	Dismissal	Friendship
Carelessness	Drink	Futility
Caution	Economy	Gambling
Change	Education	Generosity
Character	Effort	Gentleness
Charity	Egotism	God
Chastity	Eloquence	Goodness
Children	Endurance	Gossip
Choice	English, The	Gratitude
Clergy	Equality	Greed
Coincidence	Error	Grief
Comfort	Evil	Happiness
Compromise	Excused	Health
Contentment	Experience	Home

Honesty	Mother	Selfishness
Honour	Nature	Sense
Hope	Neatness	Separation
Humility	Necessity	Shame
Humour	Nobility	Shyness
Hunger	Obedience	Silence
Idleness	Obligation	Strength
Ignorance	Ownership	Stupidity
Impossibility	Participation	Success
Independence	Patience	Suitability
Inequality	Patriotism	Tact
Initiative	Peace	Talent
Intelligence	Perception	Talkativeness
Involvement	Pity	Thrift
Irishman	Poetry	Time
Judgement	Possession	Treachery
Justice	Poverty	Trouble
Kerry	Power	Trust
Kindness	Presumption	Truth
Kinship	Pride	Understanding
Knowledge	Procrastination	Uselessness
Law	Promise	Value
Laziness	Proverbs	Vanity
Leadership	Prudence	Warning
Lies	Red-hair	Wastefulness
Life	Repentance	Wealth
Love	Reputation	Weather
Luck	Revenge	Welcome
Manners	Rogue	Widow
Marriage	Rumour	Wisdom
Maturity	Scarcity	Woman
Meanness	Seasons	Work
Men	Secret	Youth
Misfortune	Self-destruction	

13

	Sparing at home and lavish in the hospital	15
	Like the sun on the hill-top, but like a thistle on the hearth	16
	Street angel, house devil	17
Age	When the twig hardens, it's difficult to twist it	18
	A man lives long in his native place	19
	It's hard to teach an old dog to dance	20

	As the cock crows, the young bird chirrups	21
	To be old and decayed dishonours no-one	22
	In youth we have our troubles before us; in age we leave pleasure behind	23
	Young people don't know what age is; old people forget what youth was	24
	The old man hasn't the place of the cat in the ashes	25
	Is it not a lonesome thing to be getting old	26
Anger	There's anger in an open laugh	27
	Old burdens don't incite blows	28
	Red-hot ashes are easily rekindled	29

	No wrong to be done to seven classes of persons excited to anger:— a bard, a chief, a woman, a prisoner, a drunken person, a druid, and a king in his own dominions	30
Appearance	An inch is a great deal in a man's nose	31
	It's not the bones that are beautiful but the flesh on the shoulders	32
	A thong is no shorter for having been in water	33
	Its appearances are better than its value	34
	Handsome is as handsome does	35
	A black hen lays white eggs	36
	A buckle is a great addition to an old shoe	37
Art	Nobility listens to art	38
As ... as	As stiff as a poker	39
	As tough as a wheelstring	40
	As mim as a dog without his tail	41
	As black as Toal's cloak	42
	As bad as Barringtons's blood hound to us	43

A localised Kerry expression. When the Irishwere being hunted down in Penal timesa particularly vicious duo, a Captain Barringtonand Colonel Nelson used a bloodhound to chasetheir quarry which savaged the victim terribly,hence giving rise to the saying.

	As old as Atty Hayes' goat	44

A Cork expression. The story goes that the goat belonged to Atwell Hayes who was father of Sir Henry Hayes, sherrif of Cork in 1790. The goat was reputed to be old even when Atty was a young man. A generation later Captain Philip Allen, son-in-law of Sir Henry Hayes became mayor of Cork, (in 1800) and gave a civil banquet to celebrate the occasion. At this time the goat died and Allen being a bit of a joker served up the hind quarters of the goat unknowingly to his guests, as venison. The 'venison' was proclaimed by the city fathers as delicious. In county Armagh the corresponding expression is 'As old as Killylea bog'.

As wise as the women of Mungret   45

A Limerick expression. The amusing story attached to this saying concerns the monastic foundation and school at Mungret. A number of scholars was sent from Cashel to compete with their Mungret counterparts. However the Limerick scholars fearing defeat and the loss of their reputation dressed as washerwomen and waited along the roadside,washing in the nearby river. As the Cashel contingent approached and asked the 'women' for directions they were completely taken aback when answered in perfect Greek. Thinking that if the washerwomen were so learned then the scholars must be unusually brilliant, the poor Tipperary monks turned for home, leaving the reputation of Mungret intact and untarnished!

As hard as the hob of hell   46

As cunning as the fox   47

As long as a wet Sunday   48

As old as the hills   49

As ... as

As melodious as a lark	70
As brave as Fionn MacCumhall (*see notes*)	71
As yellow as a ragweed (*ragworth*)	72
As lazy as a donkey	73
As lazy as a piper's luidin (*little finger*)	73a
As busy as a bee	74

As salty as the sea	75
As good as gold	76
As rich as Damer	77

A Dublin expression, not in common usage. The story is based on Joseph Damer, born in 1630. After serving Cromwell he returned to Ireland where he purchased much land forfeited in the Williamite confiscations. He became a banker and achieved much noteriety as a miser. He died in 1720 leaving nearly half a million pounds, a phenomenal amount even by to-day's standards. Johnathan Swift was moved, as was his wont, to comment unfavourably on Mr. Damer:

The ghost of old Damer who left not his betters
When it heard of a bank appear'd to his debtors
And lent them for money the backs of his letters
His debtors they wonder'd to find him so frank,
For old Nick gave the papers the mark of the bank.

	God bless three times, and three spits for luck *(said at the birth of a calf)*	95a
Boasting	There are two heads on all his sheep	96
Borrowing	The law of borrowing is to break the borrower	97
	The borrowed horse has hard hoofs	98
	The loan of something on loan	99
	Don't exchange your horse when you are crossing the river	100
	He who is bad to give the loan is good for directing you	101
Bravery	The brave man never loses	102
	Every dog is valiant at his own door	103
	Every hound is brave on his own dunghill	104
	Every man is bold until he faces a crowd	105
Bribery	Bribe the rogue and you need have no fear of the honest man	106
	Beware of the bribed man	107
	Bribery will split a stone	108
	Hold on to the bone and the dog will follow you	109
Carelessness	Loose and careless like the leg of a pot	110
	A ship is often lost because of one man	111
	By their tongues people are caught, and by their horns, cattle	112

Don't be the mean and don't be generous
with the clergy   180

The curse of Cromwell on you — 208a

Cynicism — It's a very good time if it lasts — 209

When the sky falls we'll all catch larks — 210

Danger — The man who loves danger shall perish in it — 211

No staying in dangerous roads — 212

A lion is not a safe companion for all persons — 213

A horse on a cliff or a cow in a swamp, two in danger — 213a

Death — Many a day we shall rest in the clay — 214

Death is the poor man's best physician — 215

Death doesn't come without a cause — 216

There's neither herb nor cure for death — 217

To die and to lose one's life are much the same thing 218

There'll be many a dry eye at his death — 219

There is hope from the mouth of the sea but none from the mouth of the grave — 220

A man at sea may return but not the man in the churchyard — 221

Sleep is the brother (or the image) of death — 222

One can't tell which skin will hang from
the rafter first, the old sheep's or the lamb's   223

The trace of the hand will live but
not the hand that made it   224

Death stares the old in the face and lurks behind the
backs of the young   225

Nimble as the hare is she is caught at last   226

There is many a person with a high head to-day
who will be lying lowly tomorrow   227

May God spare anyone who has a hand in his
own death   228

You will never comb a grey head   229

It is not the tree that is a long time shaking
that is the first to fall   230

Death does not take a bribe   231

The graveyard growth is in him   232

Death never comes too late   233

You'll be going yet and your two feet before you   234

	An old cat will not burn himself	315
	Sense bought (i.e. experience) is better than two senses learned	316
	You can't put an old head on young shoulders	317
	Every hound is a pup till he hunts	317a
Fair-haired	If I am yellow I have a fair heart	318
Fame	Fame lasts longer than life	319
	Without money fame is dead	320
	Falling is easier than rising	321
	Greatness knows modesty	322
Familiarity	To know somebody, (one must) live in the same house with him	323
	Too much of one thing is the same as nothing	324
	Familiarity breeds contempt	325
	People of the same trade are friendly	326
Fate	Long as the day may be night comes at last	327
	He that is born to be hanged needn't fear water	328
	Every nursling as it is nursed, every web as it is woven	329
	Pity the man drowned in the storm; for after the rain comes the sunshine	330
	The darkest hour is nearest dawn	331
	A ship is often lost by the harbour	332

	No matter how often a pitcher goes to the water, it is broken in the end	333
	No matter how long the day, night comes	334
	What kills one man gives life to another	335
	About the foot of the tree the foliage falls	336
Fear	Fear is a fine spur, so is rage	337
	Be afraid, and you'll not meet danger	338
	The man who is struck on the head, will afterwards be afraid	339
Fighting	To fight like Kilkenny cats	340

In 1798 when the Hessians were quartered in Kilkenny they amused themselves by tying two cats tails together and throwing them over a line, to fight. Their officer on hearing of this, ordered his men to stop. However the soldiers continued the practice in secret, and one day while they were amusing themselves in this manner they heard the officer approaching. One soldier drawing his sword cut down the cats leaving only their tails hanging. When the officer enquired as to where the cats were, the soldier replied that the cats had fought so furiously that they had devoured all but each other's tails. The story proved immensely popular - but it is probably just a tall tale!

	Quarrelsome dogs get dirty coats	341
	Don't kick till you're spurred	342
	Be warning but not striking	343
	A word goes to the wind but a blow goes to the bones	344
	Wine is better than blood	345
	There is often the death of a person between two words	346

Futility

Take gifts with a sigh, most men give to be paid   440

O'Neill's gift and his two eyes looking after it
(*see notes*)   441

It is worth going to meet generosity that is slow   442

Gentleness   A gentle answer quenches anger   443

A kind word never broke anyone's mouth   444

God   God's help is nearer than the door   445

God is not as severe as he is said to be   446

God often pays debts without money   447

God moves slowly yet his grace comes   448

God never closes one door but he opens another   449

God shares the good things   450

The person not taught by God is not taught by man   451

The love of God guides every good   452

	The miller's pigs are fat but God knows whose meal they ate	512
	He is as honest as the priest	513
Honour	A patch is better than a hole, but a hole is more honourable than a patch	514
	It's more difficult to maintain honour than to become prosperous	515
	A man may live after losing his life but not after losing his honour	516
	Honour is more precious than gold	517
Hope	Live horse and you'll get grass	518
	Hope soothes the tired heart	519
	Hope is the physician of each misery	520
	Face the sun but turn your back on the storm	521
	There's no flood that doesn't recede	522
	Do not expect more than you deserve	523
	God never sent a mouth without something with it	524
	The dogs have not eaten up the end of the year yet	525
	Good hope is better than a bad intention	526
	There are fish in the tide as good as any that has been taken	527
	There's fish in the sea better than was ever caught	528
	In the end the improvement comes	529
	The night and the day are as long as ever they were	530

Humility	The last place is worthy of the best loved	531
	The heaviest ear of corn is the one that lowest bends its head	532
Humour	Good humour comes from the kitchen	533
	Crying is not far away from laughter	534
Hunger	It's a good story that fills the belly	535
	Hunger is a good sauce	536
	The mountain is a good mustard	537
	The hungry hound thinks not of her whelps	538
	Sharp is the eye of the hungry person	539
	A blessing does not fill the stomach	540
Idleness	Talking never brought the turf home	541
	Don't let the grass grow under your feet	542

	Better idle than working for nothing	543
	It is better to be putting knots on a straw than to be idle	544
	A foot at rest meets nothing	545
	You have the foal's share of the harrow	546

It's only a worthless hen that fails
to provide for herself   597

The speckled shins of spring is
the envious one in Autumn   598

Laziness is a heavy burden   599

You'd be a good messenger to send for death   600

Pity the man who waits till the last day   601

Ye look for the ladle when the pot's in the fire   602

The long stitch of the lazy tailor   603

A slow messenger is the better for
your going to meet him   604

It's a bad bird that dirties its own nest   605

It's a bad hen that won't scratch herself   606

Leadership   After the chieftains fall, the fight seldom continues   607

Lies   As great a liar as the clock of Strabane   608

The lie often goes further than the truth   609

God does not like the lying tongue   610

Life   We live as long as we're let   611

You will live during the year for
we were just talking of you   612

Life is sweet   613

Life is precious   614

People live in one another's shadows   615

Twenty years agrowing; twenty years at rest; twenty years declining; and twenty years when it doesn't matter whether you're there or not	616
Life is the true historian	617

Love

Live in my heart and pay no rent	618
If you love the mother, you love her brood	619
They won't fall in love with the man they don't see	620
When the sight leaves the eye, love leaves the heart	621
After the settlement (the dowry), comes the love	622
Love is blind to blemishes and faults	623
Love hides ignominy and evil	624
Love is no impartial judge	625
House without hound, cat, or child, house without love or affection	626
Love a woman or a child without their knowing it	627
To the raven her own chick is white	628
What is nearest the heart is usually nearest the lips	629
What is nearest the heart comes out	630
Love cools quickly	631
Love conceals ugliness, and hate sees a lot of faults	632
She who fills the heart, fills the eye	633
There's no love until there's a family	634
Absence makes the heart grow fond	635

Luck	It's better to be lucky than to be an early riser	636
	A chance shot will not kill the devil	637
	The man who has luck in the morning has luck in the afternoon	638
	There's luck in sharing	639
	It's better to be lucky than wise	640
	A meeting in the sunlight is lucky, and a burying in the rain	641
	The lucky person has only to be born	642
	Luck seldom lasts	643
Manners	Without store no friends; without rearing no manners	644
	Better good manners than good looks	645
Marriage	The husband of the sloven is known in the field amidst a crowd	646
	A growing moon and a flowing tide are lucky times to marry in	647
	Never make a toil of pleasure, as the man said when he dug his wife's grave only three feet deep	648
	Marriage at the dungheap and the godparents far away	649
	Woe to him who does not heed a good wife's counsel	650

Marriage

It's why women marry — the creatures,
God bless them, are too shy to say no   651

There was never an old slipper
but there was an old stocking to match it   652

A young man is bothered till he's married,
after that he's bothered entirely   653

There's only one thing in the world
better than a good wife.....no wife   654

The dowry falls over the cliff;
but the protruding lip remains on the wife   655

A bad wife takes advice from everyone
but her husband   656

He breaks his wife's head
and then buys a plaster for it   657

There are no trials till marriage   658

The carefree mother's daughter makes a bad wife   659

It's a lonesome washing that
there's not a (man's) shirt in   660

Marry a mountainy woman and you'll marry
the mountain   661

She's a good woman, but she didn't
take off her boots yet   662

The day you marry your wife
you marry your children   663

The blanket is the warmer of being doubled   664

She burnt her coal and did not warm herself   665

	He married money and got a woman with it	666
	Marry in haste and be sorry at your leisure	667
Maturity	By age or ability you're no child	668
Meanness	What you give wouldn't blind the eye of a midge	669
	As tight as tuppence in a market-woman's trashbag	670
	If you give the loan of your britches, don't cut off the buttons	671
	'Tis strange that the man who is so quick to find fault is himself so stingy about food	672
	To come with one hand longer than the other	673
	Nothing comes into a closed hand	674
Men	Some men are like bagpipes.... they can't speak till their bellies are filled	675
Misfortune	From the house of the devil to the house of the demon	676
	After misfortune the Irishman sees his profit	677
	It is well that misfortunes come one by one and not all together	678
	It's easy to sleep on the misfortune of others	679
	When misfortune is greatest relief is nearest	680
	There's worse than this in the North	681
	Nothing is ever as bad as it seems	682
	The old white horse is the end of all misfortune	683

	He got it from nature as the pig got the rooting in the ground	697
	Often a cow does not take after its breed	698
	What would a young cat do but eat mice?	699
	Nature will come through the claws, and the hound will follow the hare	700
	If you put a silk dress on a goat he is a goat still	701
	Every bird as it is reared and the lark for the bog	702
	What is in the marrow is hard to take out of the bone	703
	The wood will renew the foliage it sheds	704
	What will come from the briar but the berry	705
	The hand goes only where the leg goes	706
Neatness	A handstaff of holly, a buailtin of hazel, a single sheaf and a clean floor *(see notes)*	707
Necessity	One who is without cows must be his own dog	708
	Make necessity a virtue	709
	Necessity accepts no law	710
	A blind man can see his mouth	711
	You never miss the water till the well has run dry	712
Nobility	A king's son is not nobler than his food (see also number 38)	713
Obedience	Keep your tongue in your jaw and your toe in your pump	714

	Time and Patience would bring the snail to Jerusalem	728
Patriotism	Everyone praises his native land	729
Peace	Nobody ever bought peace but the man who hadn't got it	730
	Peace (quietness) is worth buying	731
	The world's quiet and the pig is in the sty	732
	Least said soonest mended	733
	No matter who succeeds or fails, the peacemaker will always suffer	734
	To the fighting man peace is sure	735
	The end of a feast is better than the beginning of a fight	736
Perception	An eye is blind in another man's corner	737
	One eye in the corner is sharper than two about the house	738
Pity	He's more to be pitied than laughed at	739
	Don't tell your complaint to one who has no pity	740
Poetry	A poem ought to be well made at first, for there is many a one to spoil it afterwards	741
Possession	It's better than it's want	742
	Have it yourself, or else do without it	743
	Better the certainty of the straddle (packsaddle) than the mere loan of a saddle	744

Possession is nine-tenths of the law   745

Better own a trifle than want a great deal   746

A wren in the hand is better than a crane
to be caught   747

Possession satisfies   748

A bird in the hand is worth two in the bush   749

It's better than the loan you couldn't get   750

Half a loaf is better than no bread   751

A live dog is better than a dead lion   752

A trout in the pot is better than a salmon in the sea   753

Poverty   Put a beggar on horseback and he'll ride to hell   754

Put a beggar on horseback and he'll go on a gallop   755

Poverty parts good company   756

Poverty destroys companionship   757

Many a defect is seen in the poor man   758

It's hard to take britches off bare hips   759

The full man does not understand
the wants of the hungry   760

A little pleases a poor man   761

Poor men take to the sea; the rich to the mountains   762

Poverty creates sadness   763

Pity the man who does wrong and is poor as well   764

There is nothing in the world so poor
as going to hell   765

The thief is no danger to the beggar   766

Poverty is no shame   767

Two things that go to loss — turf on a mountain
and the wisdom of a poor man   768

Shame is ever a part of poverty   769

No-one is ever poor who has the sight of his eyes
and the use of his feet   770

There is no tune without a penny   771

A poor man never yet lost his property   772

Poor is the church without music   773

A smokey cabin, a handful of spuds and
a flea-filled bed   774

Power   No stopping the force of a going wheel by hand   775

No forcing the sea   776

Presumption   Don't count your chickens before they are hatched   777

Don't bless the fish till it gets to the land   778

Don't build the sty until the litter comes   779

Red-hair   If you meet a red-haired woman,
you'll meet a crowd   799

To be red-haired is better
than to be without a head   800

Repentance   To put off repentance is dangerous   801

It's better to be sorry and stay
than to be sorry and go away   802

Reputation   It's a small thing that outlives a man   803

Remember even if you lose all, keep your good
name for if you lose that you are worthless   804

Those who get the name of rising early
may lie all day   805

When a man gets his feet in lime
he cannot easily get rid of it   806

Revenge   No dealing with a revengeful man   807

Rogue   He was never good since the time a yard (of cloth)
made a coat for him   808

Don't mention him and a decent man in the one day   809

A sly rogue is often in good dress   810

She would drink the cream and say the cat
she had was an old rogue   811

The horse with the most scars
is the one that highest kicks his rear   812

Rumour   The person who brings a story to you
will take away two from you   813

A story without an author is not worth listening to   814

Leave the bad tale where you found it   815

There is no smoke without fire   816

*(See also **Gossip**)*

Scarcity	When all fruits fail welcome haws	817
	When the fruit is scarcest, its taste is sweetest	818
	We have a fine day more often than a kiln-cast	819
Seasons	A soft-dropping April brings milk to cows and sheep	820
	Autumn days come quickly like the running of a hound on the moor	821
	A misty winter brings a pleasant spring, a pleasant winter a misty spring	822
	Many a sudden change takes place on a spring day	823
	In winter the milk goes to the cow's horns	824
Secret	A secret is a weapon and a friend	825
	It is no secret that is known to three	826
	Fences (ditches) have ears	827

	Don't tell your secret even to a fence	828
	Woe to the man that entrusts his secrets to a ditch	829
	The secret of an old woman scolding	830
	If it's a secret, it's binding	831
	Don't tell secrets to the children of your relatives	832
Self-Destruction	No tree but has rotten wood enough to burn it	833
	A man may be his own ruin	834
	A wedge from itself splits the oak tree	835
	A man has often cut a rod to beat himself	836
Selfishness	It's for her own good that the cat purrs	837
	His own wound is what everyone feels soonest	838
	What is nearest the heart is nearest the mouth	839
	He who is best to me is he who shall get the best share	840
	The full stomach does not understand the empty one	841
	The man who was dividing Ireland didn't leave himself last	842
Sense	Sense doesn't come before age	843
Separation	After the gathering comes the scattering	844
Shame	What would shame him would turn back a funeral	845
	A fist full of gain and a village full of shame	846

	Better is the trouble that follows death than the trouble that follows shame	847
Shyness	Do not keep your tongue under your belt	848
	A man is shy in another man's corner	849
Silence	A silent mouth is musical	850
	The silent are often guilty	851
	The silent mouth is sweet to hear	852
	When wrathful words arise a closed mouth is soothing	853
	The stars make no noise	854
	Little talk is easy to cure	855
	A closed mouth — a wise head	856
	A silent mouth never did any harm	857
Strength	Strength is not enduring	858
Stupidity	Sending the goose on a message to the fox's den	859
	Putting the fox to mind the geese	860
	You didn't turn up when sense was being distributed	861
Success	There's neither success nor efficiency without authority and laws	862
	Fat is not to be had without labour	863
Suitability	The windy day is not the day for thatching	864
	One man's meat is another man's poison	865

Whoever the cap
fits takes it 866

Tact · Better sit beside
him than in his
place 867

A short visit is best and that not too often 868

The eye should be blind in the home of another 869

It's often a man's mouth broke his nose 870

Don't say everything you want to say
lest you hear something you would not like to hear 871

Don't let your tongue cut your throat 872

See not what you see and hear not what you hear 873

Never speak to the feet while the head is alive 874

Don't rest your eyes beyond what is your own 875

It's bad manners to talk about ropes in the house
of a man whose father was hanged 876

Talent · A greyhound finds food in its feet 877

The slow hound often has good qualities 878

The bird that can sing and won't sing
should be made to sing 879

A cat between two houses, a rabbit between
two holes, the two liveliest 879a

Talkativeness · Great talk and little action 880

Treachery	He who spies is the one who kills	889
	Treachery returns	890
Trouble	There's trouble in every house and some in the street	891
	Everything troubles you and the cat breaks your heart	892
Trust	The fox never found a better messenger than himself	893
	Never trust a spiteful man	894
Truth	A man with a loud laugh makes truth itself seem folly	895
	Truth is great and will win out	896
	Even the truth may be bitter	897
	There are two tellings to every story	898
	Drunkenness and anger, 'tis said tell the truth	899
	What I'm afraid to hear I'd better say first myself	900
	Truth speaks even though the tongue were dead	901
	You can keep away from the rogue, but you cannot keep yourself safe from the liar	902
	Truth stands when everything else falls	903
	It is no shame to tell the truth	904
	Tell the truth and shame the devil	905
Understanding	The well-filled belly has little understanding of the empty	906

	'Tis afterwards that everything is understood	907
Uselessness	It's a bad hound that's not worth the whistling	908
	He knows how many grains to a bushel of wheat	909
	He knows the price of everything and the value of nothing	910
	He couldn't drag a herring off the coals	911
	It's just a wisp in place of a brush	912
Value	One pair of good soles is worth two pairs of upper leathers	913
	Without pressing too little or too hard, hold tight the reins for he's a fool who would not get value from a borrowed horse	914
	It's not worth a cuckoo-spit	915
	Better an idle house than a bad tenant	916
Vanity	Pity him who makes his opinion a certainty	917
	He thinks that he himself is the very stone that was hurled at the castle	918
	He dotes on his midden and thinks it the moon	919
Warning	That's a spoon ye'll sup sorrow with yet	920
Wastefulness	Wilful waste makes woeful want	921
Wealth	A shamefaced man seldom acquires wealth	922
	The money-maker (profiteer) is never tired	923
	The doorstep of a great house is slippery	924

	There is misfortune only where there is wealth	925
	Sweet is the voice of the man who has wealth	926
	A hut is a palace to a poor man	927
	A heavy purse makes a light heart	928
	There's little value in the single cow	929
	A man of one cow – a man of no cow	930
	It's easy to knead when meal is at hand	931
Weather	Wind from the east is good for neither man nor beast	932
	A Kerry shower is of twenty-four hours	933
	Better April showers than the breadth of the ocean in gold	934
Welcome	Better for a man to have even a dog welcome him than a dog bark at him	935
	Going in is not the same as going out	936
	A welcome is a debtor's face	937
Widow	What's all the world to a man when his wife is a widow	938
Wisdom	A wise head keeps a shut mouth	939
	Everyone is wise till he speaks	940
	Food is no more important than wisdom	941
	A contraction (in writing) is enough for a scholar	942
	The beginning of wisdom is the fear of God	943

There's no wise man without a fault   944

He may die of wind but he'll never die of wisdom   945

You can't put a wise head on young shoulders   946

Wisdom is what makes a poor man a king,
a weak person powerful,
a good generation of a bad one,
a foolish man reasonable   947

Though wisdom is good in the beginning,
it is better at the end   948

A little of anything isn't worth a pin; but a wee
bit of sense is worth a lot   949

No making of a wise man   950

Women   A dishonest woman can't be kept in and an honest
         woman won't   951

There is no thing wickeder than a woman
of evil temper   952

A bad woman
(wife) drinks a lot of
her own bad
butter-milk   953

A foolish woman
knows a foolish
man's faults   954

A whistling woman
and a crowing hen
will bring no luck to
the house they are in   955

Women

Beef to the heels like a Mullingar heifer	956
Eight lives for the men and nine for the women	957
Wherever there are women there's talking, and wherever there's geese there's cackling	958
Irishwomen have a dispensation from the Pope to wear the thick ends of their legs downwards	959
Women are shy and shame prevents them from refusing a man	960
Everything dear is a woman's fancy	961
Like an Irish wolf she barks at her own shadow	962
She wipes the plate with the cat's tail	963
More hair than tit, like a mountain heifer	964
Women are stronger than men, they do not die of wisdom	965
When the old woman is hard pressed, she has to run	966
It's difficult to trust a woman	967
Man to the hills, woman to the shore	968
Beat a woman with a hammer and you'll have gold	969
'Tis as hard to see a woman cry, as a goose go barefoot	970
'Where comes a cow,' the wise man lay down (St Colmcille), 'there follows a woman, and where comes a woman follows trouble'	971
Only a fool would prefer food to a woman	972

Women

Don't be ever in court or a castle without a woman
to make your excuse   973

An excuse is nearer to a woman than her apron   974

There is nothing sharper than a woman's tongue   975

A woman without is she who has neither
pipe nor child   976

The yellow praiseach (kale) of the fields
that brings the Meath women to harm   977

A woman like a goose, a sharp pecking woman
A woman like a pig, a sleepy-headed woman
A woman like a sickle, a strong stubborn woman
A woman like a goat, a woman of rushing visits
A woman like a sheep, an affable friendly woman
A woman like a lamb, a quiet friendly woman   978

It is not the most beautiful woman
who has the most sense   979

A woman can beat the devil   980

A shrew gets her wish but suffers in the getting   981

Work

Many a time the man with ten (cows)
has overtaken the man with forty (cows)   982

Do it as if there was fire in your skin   983

The seeking for one thing will find another   984

Make your hay before the fine weather leaves you   985

Sow early and mow early   986

The early riser gets through his business
but not through early rising   987

The slow horse reaches the mill 988

Making the beginning is one third of the work 989

The quiet pigs eat all the draff 990

The sweat of one's brow is what burns everyone 991

Everyone lays a burden on the willing horse 992

Every little makes a mickle 993

Speed and accuracy do not agree 994

Never put off tomorrow what you can do today 995

I'll go there tonight for evening is speedier than morning 996

The person of the greatest talk is the person of the least work 997

Be there with the day and be gone with the day 998

About evening a man is known 999

Long churning makes bad butter 1000

Scattering is easier than gathering 1001

The labour of the crow 1002

Put it on your shoulder and say it is not a burden	1003
It's no delay to stop to edge the tool	1004
The mason who strikes often is better than the one who strikes too hard	1005
It destroys the craft not to learn it	1006
The dog that's always on the go, is better than the one that's always curled up	1007
Handfuls make a load	1008
Don't go early or late to the well	1009
A good beginning is half the work	1010

Youth

Praise the young and they will make progress	1011
Many a shabby colt makes a fine horse	1012
The young shed many skins	1013
Youth likes to wander	1014
The growth of the gosling	1015
Youth cannot believe	1016

The Triads

TRIADS

*Three
as good as*

Three things as good as the best: dirty water
to quench a fire, a frieze coat on a frosty day and
black bread in famine time.   1017

Three things that are as good as things better
than them: a wooden sword in a coward's hand,
an ugly wife married to a blind man and
poor clothes on a drunken man.   1018

Three best

Three best friends and three worst enemies:
fire, wind and rain.   1019

Three best to have in plenty:
sunshine, wisdom, and generosity.   1020

Three best things to have a surplus of:
money after paying the rent, seed after spring
and friends at home.   1021

Three best invitations: come to mass,
come and make secure and come to the mill.   1022

Three with best sight: the eye of a blacksmith
on a nail, the eye of a young girl at a contest
and the eye of a priest on his parish.   1023

Three best small:
a beehive, a sheep, and a woman.   1024

The three best sounds: the sound of the flail,
the sound of the quern, the sound of the churn.   1024a

Three fortunes The three fortunes of the cat:
the housewife's forgetfulness,
walking without a sound,
and keen sight in darkness.   1025

Three fortunes of the lucky man:
fences, vigilance, and early rising.   1026

Three fortunes of the unlucky man:
long visits to his neighbours, long morning sleep
and bad fences.   1027

Three hardest The three hardest to go through:
a waterfall, a bog and a briary track.   1028

The three hardest to select:
a Sunday woman, an autumn sheep
and an old mare's foal.   1029

Three kinds

The three kinds of brain:
brain as hard as stone,
brain as receptive as wax and
brain as unstable as flowing water.   1030

The three kinds of men:
the worker, the pleasure-seeker and the boaster. 1031

The three kinds of men who fail
to understand women:
young men, old men and
middle-aged men.   1032

The three kinds of men who rise earliest:
the husband of a talkative wife,
the man with a stolen white horse,
and the man withthe dirty tattered shirt.   1033

The three kinds of poor people:
the man poor by the will of God,
the man poor by his own will and
the man poor even if he owned the world.   1034

The three kinds of women: the woman as
shameless as a pig: the woman as unruly as a hen
and the woman as gentle as a lamb.   1035

Three most

The three most bothersome things in the world:
a thorn in the foot, a woman and a goat going
to the fair that will go anyway but
the way you want it.   1036

The three most delightful things to see:
a garden of white potatoes covered in blossom,
a ship under sail and a woman after giving birth.   1037

The three most difficult to select:
a woman, a scythe and a razor.   1038

The three most difficult to teach:
a mule, a pig and a woman.   1039

The three most difficult to understand:
the mind of a woman, the labour of the bees
and the ebb and flow of the tide.   1040

The three most fortunate things a man ever had:
a mare, a sow and a goose.   1041

The three most nourishing foods: beef marrow,
the flesh of a chicken, Scandinavian beer.   1042

The three most pleasant things:
a cat's kitten, a goat's kid and
a young widow-woman.   1043

The three most troubled eyes:
the eye of a blacksmith after the nail,
the eye of a chicken after the grain and
the eye of a girl seeking her sweetheart.   1043a

Three traits

Three traits of a bull:
a bold walk, a strong neck and a hard forehead.   1044

Three traits of a fox:
a light step, a look to the front and
a glance to each side of the road.   1045

Three traits of a hare:
a lively ear, a bright eye and
a quick run against the hill.   1046

Three traits of a woman:
a broad bosom, a slender waist and a short back.   1047

Three ugliest

The three ugliest things that are:
a hairless mangy dog,
a woman without flesh or blood,
and a deceitful, shameless girl.   1048

The three ugliest things of their own kind:
a thin red-haired woman,
a thin yellow horse and a thin white cow.   1049

Three useless

The three things useless when old:
an old schoolmaster, an old horse
and an old soldier.   1050

Three things that are of little use:
a trumpet and no tongue,
a button and no buttonhole
and a wolf without teeth.   1051

Three worst

The three worst departures:
leaving mass before it ends,
leaving table without grace and
leaving your wife to go to another woman.   1052

The three worst endings:
the last days of a noble old lady,
the last days of an old white horse
and the last days of an old schoolmaster   1053

The three worst endings: a house burning;
a ship sinking and an old white horse dying.   1053a

The three worst pets:
a pet priest, a pet beggar and a pet pig.   1054

The three worst things to have in a house:
a scolding wife, a smokey chimney and a leaky roof. 1055

The three worse things of all: small, soft potatoes,
from that to an uncomfortable bed and
to sleep with a bad woman.   1056

Three things The things that cannot be acquired:
voice, generosity and poetry.   1057

Three things that arrive unnoticed:
rent, age and a beard.   1058

Three things to beware of: the hoof of the horse,
the horn of the bull and the smile of the Saxon.   1059

Three things a man should not boast of:
the size of his purse, the beauty of his wife
and the sweetness of his beer.   1060

Three things bright at first, then dull and
finally black: co-operation, a marriage alliance
and living in the one house.   1061

Three things Christ never intended: a woman
whistling, a hound howling and a hen crowing.   1062

Three Things

Three things that relate to drink:
to pay for it, to drink it and to carry it.   1063

Three things that fill a haggard:
ambition, industry and constant vigilance.   1064

Three good things to have: a clean shirt,
a clean conscience and a guinea in the pocket.   1065

Three disagreeable things at home:
a scolding wife, a squalling child
and a smoky chimney.   1066

Three things that don't bear nursing:
an old woman, a hen and a sheep.   1067

Three things that are purposeless:
throwing a stone on a bend,
giving advice to a wrathful woman,
talking to a head without sense.   1068

Three things that remain longest in a family:
fighting, red-hair and thieving.   1069

Three things that don't remain: a white cow,
a handsome woman and a house on a height.   1070

Three things that can never return: a Sunday
without mass, a day away from school and
a day away from work.   1071

Three things that won't have rest: a steep
waterfall, an otter and a devil out of hell.   1072

Three things that never rust:
a woman's tongue,
the shoes of a butcher's horse and
charitable people's money.   1073

Three Things

Three things that never rust:
a sword, a spade and a thought. 1074

Three things never seen:
a blade's edge, wind and love. 1075

Three sharpest things that are: a hound's tooth,
a thorn in the mud and a fool's word. 1076

The three sharpest things:
a fool's word, a thorn in the mud
and a soft woollen thread that cuts to the bone. 1077

Three things that survive for the shortest time:
a woman's association, the love of a mare
for her foal and fresh oaten bread. 1078

Three thing swiftest in the sea:
the seal, the ray and the mackerel. 1079

Three things swiftest on land:
the hound, the hare and the fox. 1080

Three things that leave the shortest traces:
a bird on a branch, a ship on the sea
and a man on a woman. 1081

Three things that leave the longest traces:
charcoal on wood, a chisel on a block of stone
and a ploughshare on a furrow.   1082

Three things not to be trusted:
a fine day in winter, the life of an old person
or the word of an important man unless it's in
writing.   1083

Three things not be trusted:
a cow's horn, a dog's tooth and a horse's hoof.   1084

Three things of least value in any house:
too many geese in a house without a lake,
too many women in a house without wool
to be spun, too many horses in a house
without ploughing to be done.   1085

Three things that have little value:
the head of a woodcock, the head of a goat
and the head of a gurnet.   1086

Three things a man should not be without:
a cat, a chimney and a housewife.   1087

Miscellaneous   Three parts of the body most easily hurt:
the knee, the elbow and the eye.   1088

Three that do not clean their snouts:
the farmer, the dog and the pig.   1089

Three coldest things that are:
a hound's snout, a man's knee
and a woman's breast.   1090

Three to whom it's little sense to pay a compliment:
an old man, a bad man and a child.   1091

Miscellaneous

Three deaths that ought not be bemoaned:
the death of a fat hog, the death of a thief
and the death of a proud prince.   1092

Three the devil has without much trouble:
the mason, the bailiff and the miller.   1093

Three enemies of the body: wind, smoke and fleas.   1094

Three errors relating to corn: to cut it green,
to grind it damp and to eat it fresh.   1095

Three great evils: smallness of house,
closeness of heart and shortage of food.   1096

Three with the sharpest eyes:
a hawk on a tree, a fox in a glen,
a young girl at a meeting.   1097

Three wholesome foods for the driver:
the back of a herring, the belly of a salmon
and the head of a thrush (moorhen).   1098

Three bad habits:
drinking the glass, smoking the pipe
and scattering the dew late at night.   1099

Three happiest in the world:
the tailor, the piper and the goat.   1100

Three strokes that are keeping Ireland:
the stroke of an axe on a block,
of a hammer on an anvil
and of a threshing flail in the centre.   1101

Three jobs that must be done with vigour:
 rowing, hammering and measuring the ground
with your fist *(ie. using the sickle)*.   1102

Miscellaneous

Three kind acts unrequited:
that done for an old man, for a wicked person
or for a little child.   1103

Three sweetest melodies: the churning of butter,
the plough ploughing and the mill grinding.   1104

Three oaths that money swore:
that it did not care who would possess it,
that it would stay but a while with any man
and that it would not stay with any man but the
man who loved it.   1105

Three pair that never agree:
two married women in the same house,
two cats with one mouse
and two bachelors after the one young woman.   1106

Three places that cannot be avoided:
the place of birth, the place of death
and the place of burial.   1107

Three times it is most likely to rain:
early on Friday, late on Saturday and
on Sunday morning when it's time for first mass.   1108

Three greatest rushes: the rush of water,
the rush of fire and the rush of falsehood.   1109

Three sauciest by nature: a ram, a bull and a tailor.   1110

Three skills of the hare: sharp turning,
high jumping, and strong running against the hill.   1111

Three strongest forces: the force of fire,
the force of water and the force of hatred.   1112

Three truths: sunrise, sunset and death.   1113

Miscellaneous

Three unluckiest things to meet first thing in the morning: a mad dog, a man who lent you money and a red-haired girl.   1114

Three virtues of the drunkard: a miserable morning, a dirty coat and an empty pocket.   1115

Three signs of an unfortunate man: going bail, intervening in disputes and giving evidence.   1115a

The three characteristics of the Fianna: purity of heart: strength of limb, and acting according to our word.   1115b

Four ...

Four priests who are not greedy: four Frenchmen who are not yellow (cowardly); four cobblers who don't tell lies; that's twelve not in this country.   1116

Four things an Irishman should not trust: a cow's horn, a horse's hoof, a dog's snarl and an Englishman's laugh. *(Compare 1059)*   1117

The four fortunes of the cat: the housewife's error: walking without care; no water in milk, and sight at night as well as by day. *(Compare 1025)*   1118

Four hateful things: a worthless hound, a slow horse, a chief without wisdom and a wife without children.   1119

NOTES

Proverbs 50 & 70 The buailtin is part of the flail that strikes the corn.

Proverb 51 Ciotog is the Irish word for a left-handed person; it often implies awkwardness. In this instance, however, the implication is one of the cuteness or guile. Various superstitions are associated with the ciotog – including suspicion of evil or treachery (note the English word 'sinister', from the latin).

Proverb 55 The Irish word 'meitheal' means a team of workers (neighbours) assisting one another at turf-cutting or hay-making. The blacksmith usually had the largest meitheal in the parish since his work at the forge was of such importance to the community.

Proverb 60 'The Old Woman of Beare' – a legendary figure in Irish folklore and poetry. (See Padraic Pearse's poem, *Mise Eire*, and Austin Clarke's, *The Young Woman of Beare*).

Proverb 71 About 300 a.d. when Corman MacArt was High King of Ireland, ruling from Tara, a warrior army called the Fianna was formed under the leadership of Fionn MacCumhaill. Around the Fianna and its leader grew a great body of legend still popular today. Fionn himself was noted for his bravery and wisdom (he tasted the salmon of knowledge). The Fianna eventually became too powerful for the High King but were defeated at the battle of Gabhra and disbanded.

Proverb 203a   The word 'cess', according to P.W. Joyce, may mean a contraction of success, or a 'contribution'. He refers to its use in County Louth as meaning a quantity of corn in for threshing.

Proverb 271   Lough Sheelin is a large lake in County Cavan

Proverb 441   Used as a reply when you are reminded by someone of a favour he has granted you.

Proverb 595 & 598   'Speckled' refers to the 'heat-spots' got on the shins from sitting too long and too close by the fire.

Proverb 716   This proverb is King Diarmuid's famous judgement, given about 560 a.d., on the ownership of a manuscript copy made by St Colmcille of a manuscript belonging to St Finnian. It must be one of our first copyright laws.

Index of Key Words

Find (to) 312

Finger 73a, 162, 485

Fire 119, 131, 186, 387, 469, 484, 816, 983, 1017, 1019, 1109, 1112

Fireside 509

First 118, 120, 123, 161, 230, 353

Fish 527-28, 778

Fist 86, 147, 554, 846, 1102

Fit (to) 866

Flail 1024a, 1101

Flattery 348

Flea 410, 774, 1094

Flesh 32, 1042, 1048

Flimsiness 349

Flock 389, 497

Flood 130, 522, 797

Floor 707

Flower 59

Foal 546, 1029, 1078

Foliage 336, 704

Follow (to) 109, 700, 847

Folly 371, 895

Fond 635

Food 182, 350-55, 550, 672, 713, 877, 941, 972, 1042, 1096, 1098

Fool 8, 12, 56, 356-67, 914, 972, 1076-77

Foolishness 160, 283, 368-72

Foot 165, 234, 256, 288, 311, 336, 489, 542, 545, 648, 770, 806,

874, 877, 1036

Forebearance 722

Force 775, 1112

Ford 130, 312, 781, 797

Forehead 1044

Forever 455

Forget (to) 24, 236, 390, 472

Forgetfulness 1025

Forgiveness 373

Fortunate 1041, 1115a

Fortune 374-381, 1025-1027, 1118

Four 1116-1119

Fox 47, 77a, 198, 859-60, 893, 1045, 1080, 1097

Frail 382

Freedom 383-84

Frenchmen 1116

Fresh 61, 1095

Friar 152, 172

Friday 1108

Friend 385, 391-392, 394, 398, 405, 415-416, 644, 825, 1019, 1021

Friendly 326, 978

Friendship 385-417

Frieze 1017

Front 114

Frosty 1017

Fruit 549, 817-818

Full 135, 183, 473, 476

Funeral 845

Furrow 1082

Futility 418-432

Gain 846

Gallop 755

Gamble (to) 433-435

Game 194

Gander 294

Garden 1037

Gathering 844, 1001

Generation 947

Generosity 180,436-42, 571, 1020, 1057

Gentleness 124, 443,-444, 1035

Gift 440-441, 471

Girl 68, 165, 1023, 1043a, 1097, 1114

Give (to) 335, 360

Glass 1099

Glen 1097

Goat 44, 170, 424, 701, 978, 1036, 1043, 1086, 1100

Gobadan 7

God 86-87, 95a, 228, 250, 445-458, 475, 512, 524, 610, 651, 943, 1034

Godparents 649

Gold 76, 361, 405, 934, 969

Good 76, 144, 148, 150-151, 153, 450, 452, 837, 1017-1018, 1065

Goodness 459-465

Goose 156, 174, 294, 693, 859, 860, 958, 970, 978, 1041, 1085

Gosling 1015

Gospel 66

Gossip 466-69

Security 574

See 115, 163, 711, 873, 1075

Seed 1021

Seek (to) 984, 1043a

Seldom 239

Select (to) 1029, 1038

Self-destruction 833-836

Selfishness 837-842

Sell (to) 198, 458, 481

Sense 316, 372, 843, 861, 949, 979, 1068

Separation 402, 844

Settlement 622

Severe 446

Shabby 1012

Shadow 615, 962

Shake 230

Shallow 240

Shame 727, 767, 769, 845-847, 904-905, 960

Shamefaced 922

Shameless 269, 1035, 1048

Share 185, 546, 639, 840

Sharp 51, 56-57, 539, 975, 1076-1077

Sheaf 707

Shed (to) 1013

Sheep 96, 349, 389, 560, 690, 820, 978, 1024, 1029, 1067

Shilling 551

Shin 126, 595, 598

Ship 111, 332, 494, 1037, 1081

Shirt 660, 1033, 1065

Shoe 37, 309, 1073

Shop 262

Shore 968

Short 257, 314

Shot 637

Shoulders 32, 317, 416, 595, 946, 1003

Shout 466

Show (to) 242

Shower 933-34

Shrew 981

Shy 651, 810, 849, 960

Shyness 848-849

Sickle 978

Sickness 493

Side 296, 398

Sigh 440

Sight 621, 770, 1023, 1025, 1118

Signify (to) 585

Sign 1115a

Silence 850-57

Silk 701

Sin 787

Sing (to) 879

Single 929

Sink (to) 1053a

Sit (to) 399, 470, 867

Skill 1111

Skin 80, 196, 198, 223, 407, 689, 983, 1013

Sky 210

Slate 370

Sleep 222, 492, 494, 596,

679, 1027, 1056

Sleepy-head 978

Slender 1047

Slip 297

Slipper 652

Slippery 924

Sloven 646

Slow 63, 311, 422, 878

Small 1024

Smile 1059

Smear (to) 301

Smith 55

Smoke 816,1094

Smoke (to) 1099

Smoky 774, 1055, 1066

Snail 727

Snarl 1117

Snout 77a, 1089-1090

Soft 348

Soldier 1050

Sole 256, 913

Somebody 323

Son 160, 162, 167, 364, 434, 713

Soon 138, 733

Soothe (to) 519, 784, 853

Sores 724

Sorrow 160, 266, 490, 685, 920

Sorry (to be) 122, 802, 667

Sound 1024a, 1025

Sour 264

Source 281

Sow 395, 986, 1041